Jilly and Jett

Guess what? Aunt Jilly is coming to my house today.

We love to color together. Jilly is a real, official artist, and she says I’m an artist, too.

I’m waiting in my cozy corner for her to get here. I’m so excited!

Jilly walks in and says, "Jett and Jilly!"

"Jilly and Jett!" I say back.

We say that every time we see each other. I run to give her a hug and we hold it for ten seconds.

Jilly says that makes our hug stick.

"I brought some sidewalk chalk today," Jilly says.

"How much driveway do you think we can cover with our art?"

"The whole thing!" I shout.

Jilly and I go outside and get started.

She draws a bright green lily pad with a frog sitting on top.

Frogs are my favorite.

I draw shapes and squiggly lines with rainbow colors.

Jilly says real art doesn't have to look like real life.

After we've been working for a while, Jilly says, "Shall we go inside and have some lunch?"

"Yes," I say. "Grilled cheese, please!"

"Let's race," Jilly says. "I'm going to get to the door first!" She starts to run.

"No you're not!" I say. Jilly is fast, but I can catch up.

When I get inside, I run to the window and look out at our colorful driveway.

I love the art we made.

I want to keep it forever.

While we're eating our lunch, we talk about colors and shapes and something called inspiration.

"Inspiration is when you're all filled up with an idea you can't wait to try out," Jilly says.

I know that feeling. "I can't wait to draw a frog on the driveway when we go back outside," I say.

Then I hear something.

I look at Jilly, and Jilly looks at me.

"It's raining," we say at the same time.

I know what to do. I hurry to the closet, grab our biggest umbrella, and run as fast as I can out to the driveway.

I hold the umbrella over our art, but the rain washes most of it away.

I can't protect it.

I am so mad. "You **naughty** clouds!"
I shout at the sky.

"Look what you did! You ruined it!"

I stomp around the driveway, making **BIG** splashes in the puddles.

My pants get soaking wet.

I sit down on the driveway and make my **grumpiest** face at the clouds.

Jilly brings me a big towel and wraps it around my shoulders.

"This is such a bummer," she says. "Let's go inside and get you some dry clothes. There's nothing more we can do here."

"Aren't you mad at the rain too, Jilly?" I ask. "It ruined everything!"

"I’m certainly disappointed," says Jilly, sitting down on the front step.

"Did stomping in the puddles help you get your feelings out?" Jilly asks. "Moving my body always helps me when I'm upset."

"I guess so." I say. Knowing that Jilly understands makes me feel a little bit better.

I change into some dry clothes, and Jilly and I go over to my cozy corner.

"This is a really nice spot," Jilly says. "Is it okay if I pull you in for a cuddle?"

I nod, and we sit in silence for a while. Jilly is good at knowing when I want to talk and when I need to just be quiet.

"This looks intriguing," Jilly says, picking up my Calming Circle. "Will you tell me about it?"

I show her how it works. We breathe together, in and out, rolling the little balls back and forth in their loop.

"Imagine that your body is full of little jumping frogs," says Jilly.

"Each time you breathe out, one of the little frogs falls asleep on its own lily pad."

I lean back against her and imagine the little frogs falling asleep, one by one.

"That rain was really disappointing," Jilly says.

I nod and say quietly, "I miss our special driveway."

"I miss it too," says Jilly. "I wonder if there's a way we can remember it."

I think for a minute. Then, I jump up and run over to my art box. "Paper!" I shout.

JETT'S
Cozy